American Sonnets

American Sonnets

Poems

Gerald Stern

W. W. NORTON & COMPANY

NEW YORK ★ LONDON

Poems in this volume have appeared or will appear in the following journals: *American Poetry Review:* "How a Word Can Breathe," "First Light," "Flexible Flyer," "The Inkspots," "Peaches," "Exordium and Terminus," "Justice," "All I Did for Him," "Crosshatching," "String Bean," "Savel Kliatchko," "Samaritan," "Egg"; *The New Yorker:* "Winter Thirst," "Aberdeen Proving Grounds, 1946," "Alone," "Apocalypse"; *Ploughshares:* "Salt"; *Poetry:* "Box of Cigars," "In Time," "Pag," "1940 LaSalle"; *Five Points:* "Dandelions," "Iris," "Studebaker"; *Iowa Review:* "Hydrangea," "Large Pots"; *Slate:* "Les Neiges d'Antan," "Grass and Water"; *Witness:* "For the Bee," "Spider"; *Yale Review:* "You"; *Field:* "Burning," "Roses"; *The Forward:* "Sam and Morris."

For information about permission to reproduce selections from this book, write to Permissions, W. W. Norton & Company, Inc., 500 Fifth Avenue, New York, NY 10110

The text of this book is composed in Columbus MT
Composition by Adrian Kitzinger
Manufacturing by The Courier Companies, Inc.
Book design by Brooke Koven
Production manager: Andrew Marasia

Library of Congress Cataloging-in-Publication Data

Stern, Gerald, date.
American sonnets : poems / Gerald Stern.
p. cm.
ISBN 0-393-05084-X
1. Sonnets, American. I. Title.
PS3569. T3888 A8 2002
811'.54—dc21

2001055765

W. W. Norton & Company, Inc., 500 Fifth Avenue,
New York, N.Y. 10110
www.wwnorton.com

W. W. Norton & Company Ltd., Castle House, 75/76 Wells Street,
London W1T 3QT

1 2 3 4 5 6 7 8 9 0

For my grandmother, Libby, and for Anne Marie

Contents

Winter Thirst   11

How a Word Can Breathe   12

June   13

Once   14

Aberdeen Proving Grounds, 1946   15

For the Bee   16

Alone   17

September, 1999   18

Rebecca   19

My Tenderness   20

You   21

First Light   22

My Stick   23

Flexible Flyer   24

Beechview   25

The Inkspots   26

Peaches   27

Exordium and Terminus   28

Bruce   29

Grass and Water   30

In Time   31

Les Neiges d'Antan   32

Sink   33

Mimi   34

All I Did for Him   35

Places You Wouldn't Believe   36

Pag   37

Hydrangea   38

Crosshatching   39

Spider   40
Dandelions   41
Hats   42
String Bean   43
Large Pots   44
Savel Kliatchko   45
Irishry   46
1940 LaSalle   47
Blue Sheets   48
Iris   49
Grand Hotel   50
Apocalypse   51
Sam and Morris   52
Burning   53
Studebaker   54
Standing Up   55
Cost   56
Still Burning   57
Samaritans   58
Roses   59
Letters   60
The Hammer   61
Hearts   62
Ted Rosenberg   63
Slash of Red   64
Salt   65
Egg   66
Box of Cigars   67
Justice   68
American Heaven   69

American Sonnets

Winter Thirst

I grew up with bituminous in my mouth
and sulfur smelling like rotten eggs and I
first started to cough because my lungs were like cardboard;
and what we called snow was gray with black flecks
that were like glue when it came to snowballs and made
them hard and crusty, though we still ate the snow
anyhow, and as for filth, well, start with
smoke, I carried it with me I know everywhere
and someone sitting beside me in New York or Paris
would know where I came from, we would go in for dinner—
red meat loaf or brown *choucroute*—and he would
guess my hill, and we would talk about soot
and what a dirty neck was like and how
the white collar made a fine line;
and I told him how we pulled heavy wagons
and loaded boxcars every day from five
to one A.M. and how good it was walking
empty-handed to the no. 69 streetcar
and how I dreamed of my bath and how the water
was black and soapy then and what the void
was like and how a candle instructed me.

How a Word Can Breathe

I don't know who said first the hardened beetle
and who was in the sun and therefore divided
the world in two and how we fixed the height
of the oak at sixty feet or who first saw
the perfect crab and counted his legs and turned him
over to see the dead man's face imprinted
on every one as long as you saw the two holes
as eyes and paid attention to the crease
that went from forehead to chin; and who remembered
the butterfly bush and actually put on his shoes
to see what color it was and who remembered
what year the Buick was and if there was a
strip in the windshield or not; and how you had to
"slay a worm"—for immortality—
and what it was like changing a bald tire,
turning the iron with your knees, holding the jack
in one of your bleeding hands, and what a "homely
anguish" is and how a word can breathe
and what the pink sky looked like with long streaks
of lavender at the edge when you looked up
from tightening the lugs and how you waited.

June

Since it is June already I could be back there
wearing a yellow hat to confuse the blue jay
or giving into the smells; and once the heat
lets up I could be shivering in a T-shirt,
wishing I had a wool sweater, remembering
the bricks in this room and how we hated plaster
yet how we painted them white and how advanced
we felt when we finally had a telephone;
and I could be picking phlox by pulling the low-lying
roots and stop to think if there could be pomp
enough with only a single four-pointed star;
and I could bend down again for the chicory
that sky and land conspired so much with it caught
the sun for a minute, and put it over my sink,
the way we brought something into the house
that we could cut the dead leaves from and water,
now that we had a well, now that the wind
was breaking down the door and one of the old
zinc pennies was standing on end and we could find
the key inside the crock, now we had light.

Once

Once I called my former wife from one of the
pay phones they used to have on the wall here
to ask her where the hospital was since I was
so overcome with fear walking down the
empty sidewalk or into one of the stores that
used to be here I couldn't tell which hill I
took though I had been there maybe a half
dozen times but she was merciless and
full of ridicule, such was my happy
marriage then, though I still tried explaining
how when I walked into Woolworth's the rubber
tiles rose up and I was half-blind and hung
onto the glass case for balance which she
interpreted as either sugar or eyeglasses;
and I remember we drove to a doctor but I was
better by then, my heart wasn't pounding, the blood
wasn't rushing into my ears, and I expanded
while paying the bill and putting my jacket on
since one more time I fought off the rubber floor
and caved-in sidewalk without disgracing myself.

Aberdeen Proving Grounds, 1946

I have had the honor of being imprisoned, the
joy of breaking stone with a sledge hammer, the
pleasure of sleeping under a bare lightbulb, the
grief of shitting with a guard watching, the
sorrow of eating by myself, and I have
felt the lightness of being released and watched the
leaves change color from a speeding car,
and I first read the Gospels then, a stiff
and swollen paperback, the way paper
was made then, and I slept peacefully,
a blanket over the steel, as I recall,
though I planned the same murder every night,
which kept me going my thirteen working hours;
and when I got home I threw my duffel bag into
the river and walked to the no. 69 streetcar,
and even the clothes I wore, even the shoes,
even the overcoat, I stuffed into
the hot incinerator and listened to the roar
three stories down and watched the particles float
inside the chute and read an old newspaper
on top of the bundle and tested the cord and cleaned
the greasy window, since I was cleaning everything.

For the Bee

The fence itself can't breathe, jewelweeds are choking
the life out of the dirt, not one tomato plant
can even survive, the crows are leaving, the worms
themselves won't stay, the bricks are hot, the water
in one of my buckets has disappeared, and I
am trying to get a pencil out of my pocket
without breaking the point though it is painful
turning sideways in this heat and lifting my
leg like that; and there is a half-dead bee
drowning in my saucer and there is a dirty
kitchen window in which I sit in front of
a piece of rough slate and hold my book to the light
like someone under a tree and nod with tears
of mercy—for the bee I guess—and stare
and frown by turns and turn my head to the tree
so I can be kind and let the filtered light
go in and out and wave a little because of the
glass the way I do when I am facing
myself in the mirror and not even ridicule
the new president and not even loathe him.

Alone

I was alone and I could do what I wanted—
I couldn't believe my luck—if I wanted to sleep
at ten in the morning I could sleep or two
in the afternoon, if that was my time, or wander
by car or foot delicately in the night
when everything was resting exhausted and stop to
eat in quiet, no humor at last, oh coffee,
coffee, I was sitting alone at a counter—
I was in a painting sort of—closeness
closer than love between me and the waitress,
and when I paid the bill more closeness; I walked
from window to window, once I walked the length
of Amsterdam Avenue, once I walked from Lake
Garda to Venice, a hundred miles, and Venice
south to Florence, through Bologna; I ate
mortadella cheap I washed in the fountains
I slept with the barking dogs and twice in my life
I woke up surrounded, once on the floor of a train station,
once on the floor of a bank. I left at five
or six in the morning; I put my keys in a bottle;
I wore two pair of socks and hid my money.

September, 1999

I was thinking about pears—or you were—I
don't remember who first started to think,
though you said Seckle pears and I said Bartlett
and nothing I could do could budge you; I
could cut the skin so quickly and keep it so thin
the light goes through it, and I held it to the light
to catch the rose, and I knew when the core was
already brown and it was spreading just by
touching the flesh, and sometimes the neck was gone,
as far as eating, though you would call it the nose,
you with your Seckles, you with your freckles, and no one
but me has quite such pleasure extruding the stem,
and no one I know puts a pear in his coat pocket
when he goes out in the rain, as I do, though what
was the pleasure eating in sheets of water compared to
the loneliness eating by yourself, and even though
hornets were in your bowl and ten or twenty
were crawling over a rotten peach and three or
four were already after my pear since it was
autumn again and hornets were dying and they were
angry, and drunk, I just wiped them away.

Rebecca

It was Jane Miller who called my lips beautiful
but that was only because she was comparing me
to my darling Rebecca who has a mouth like a
red peach, a red finch, a salmon,
who lay beside me amused and puzzled with her
small head drawn back taking part of the world
in the way her great-great-grandfather did in
Poland and her great-great-grandmother in Pennsylvania
as they stood there charily waiting for her birth
oh a century ago, the one of them looking into
a steaming marsh, one of them walking through
a frozen valley, for all I know their lips
beautiful too; and I can't wait till she is
old enough to root through some pictures she
will find in her mother's house or Anne Marie's house
and spread them out on the floor, something from
Prague, of course, or something from the wedding,
me with a broken shoulder in a black
tuxedo, ridiculous naturally in her day,
but maybe touching that she could sit down and stare at
or hold against her cheek her first trip east.

My Tenderness

One good sneeze deserves another, one good
stroke, one heart attack, since everything
comes in twos—I die for example if I don't
touch a door a second time, a brick wall, a
tree, or take my steps between the cracks, not
counting buckles, which is why I went crazy
walking with minced steps on the railroad ties
north of Governor Street in Iowa City
where I lived for nine years since there's no sense
pretending they come in twos—the rails themselves,
they come in twos—and God knows I couldn't hop
from rail to rail and I couldn't make my strides
that wide, leaving only the weeds below
and sky above, which after a while I saw was
the root to what I suffered from, trying to
bring them together; you'd have to leave Pennsylvania
and live in Iowa to see the separation
and know what a struggle it was to make the two
one, for which my humor was only an
endearment, maybe even my tenderness.

You

You know my story better than I do and if
I stray a little you will correct me but more
like a child corrects his mother, entwined as they are,
when even a word is mispronounced or some
small detail is passed over, especially
how many teeth were in a mouth or what
the name of the wolf was—or the green spider—
only for once it is smells we are talking about
and I am trying to describe a fragrance
by using words and I try desperately
to do it, and you nod by way of agreement,
knowing how difficult and even ridiculous
it is and we both know that only by likeness
can we be near, comparison I should say,
and both of us struggle to describe the smell of
snow in 1940, mixed as it was with
coal fumes and the rawness of locusts in that
foggy mountain climate and an air
explosive with dust and dirt from the steel mills rising
like orange fat for the gods, though you weren't born yet.

First Light

Sooner or later everyone's eyes are opened
though it is the pain of light for the first one out
I have the most pity for, his voice shaking, the
beams mostly in vertical lines, the daylight
above the wooded hills most critical,
seen as it is through two French doors, a clock
of crazy birds to the right, a rufous-sided towhee,
a whooping crane, an eastern bluebird, North
American birds—on the hour—singing and calling,
whatever they do, though I can see me sitting
inside a house, and how the horizon line,
given the window, is higher, and if it turns out
we were in a valley and those were mountains,
how dark it was and how I'd have to stretch
to see what's left of the light, for all of life
is lowered like that, you start with a brutal lamp
and so on and so on—I would have a hard time
explaining what was opened in my life
and what was destroyed, and how the streaks mattered.

My Stick

My stick was maybe five foot tall and perfectly
curved for my hand, on either side, with just a
touch of the bark so I could work my nervousness
out by doing a little stripping the way I
do on plastic bottles, keeping the paper
attached till the last minute and scraping the glue
with one of my thumbs, the label over my hand
and resting on my knuckles, the two knots
like great knobs, like knees even, the tip
barely split, a darkness where the rain
almost never stopped and fuzziness—
practically fur—along an aborted branch,
between the legs you might say, well, a general
softness, a dryness, to the stick, a reticence
sort of, I want to say pity or mercy but
that's not the point, the stick, after all, is made
for other things, kind stick; throwing it away,
tossing it into a river or over a tree,
that's only love, that's only insanity.

Flexible Flyer

The tale I have to tell. I lit a match
outside in the snow, it was a homemade firebox
abounding in rust; when we came down the blaze
itself was gone but there were black sticks mixed
with the fiery wood and three or four potatoes
were mixed in with the sticks so you could eat
one potato or the other, and in the
clarity around us you could feed
either way on fire; the long climb up
was over a mile—I never for a minute
groaned or counted my steps but I knew trees
on both sides of the road and metal sewers
filled with slippery leaves. One way there was
nothing sort of, only the smoking firebox
when you looked back; the other way the gloomy
perfect light—I can't remember now
which of the two, I think it was a mixture—
and ice formed on our eyelids I remember,
at least on mine I know, and for a second,
before I blinked I doubled my vision and since
the snow was blue I washed my face in lavender.

Beechview

No one would believe what it was like
then, everyone had a hill and the snow
piled up so high you left your car at the bottom
in front of someone else's house and there was
a window I drew on and there was a door
that kept the snow at bay and I drove back
forty years later and the woods were gone
and there were small ugly houses everywhere;
and I was followed by a police car because I
made the mistake of slowing down in front of
the house I thought was mine but I couldn't see
the two peach trees so I wasn't sure or the
cement urns or the door oddly to the right
when I looked up on the porch and there was the window
I longed for, there were two but it was the one
on the left away from the door, though it was summer
when I came back, and I was against sullenness
so I drove the car in low, nodding and smiling,
talking to no one near me, turning left
on the first street, right on the next, swine behind me.

The Inkspots

The thing about the dove was how he cried in
my pocket and stuck his nose out just enough to
breathe some air and get some snow in his eye and
he would have snuggled in but I was afraid
and brought him into the house so he could shit on
the *New York Times,* still I had to kiss him
after a minute, I put my lips to his beak
and he knew what he was doing, he stretched his neck
and touched me with his open mouth, lifting
his wings a little and readjusting his legs,
loving his own prettiness, and I just
sang from one of my stupid songs from one of my
vile decades, the way I do, I have to
admit it was something from *trains.* I knew he'd like that,
resting in the coal car, slightly dusted with
mountain snow, somewhere near Altoona,
the horseshoe curve he knew so well, his own
moan matching the train's, a radio
playing the Inkspots, the engineer roaring.

Peaches

What was I thinking of when I threw one of my
peach stones over the fence at Metro North,
and didn't I dream as always it would take
root in spite of the gravel and the newspaper,
and wasn't I like that all my life, and who isn't?
I thought of oranges and, later, watermelon
and yellow mangoes hanging from sweetened strings,
but it was peaches, wasn't it, peaches most of
all I thought about and if the two trees that
bore such hard little fruit would only have lived
a few years more how I would have had a sister
and I would have watched her blossom, her brown curls
her blue eyes, though given her family she would have
been wild and stubborn, harsh maybe, she would
be the angry one—how quiet I was—the Chinese
grew their peaches for immortality—the
Russians planted theirs so they could combine
beauty and productivity, that was
my aesthetic too, I boiled my grape leaves,
I ate my fallen apples, loving sister.

Exordium and Terminus

In your rendition of *The Year 25-25*
the airplane rattles, the engine roars, the sardines
around me smile, like sardines, and you kiss me
twice, once on the cheek and once on the ear.
It is a song from 1965–1970;
some keeper of music will know the title, the singer,
where it was on the charts, what it reflects
of what was Doomsday then and how long it stayed
in the top ten or twenty. And who was president,
whether he had a girlfriend, whether J. Edgar
was still around and whether or not his boyfriend
ate cottage cheese like him. And what I was doing,
and what car I was driving, and how much money I
owed to banks, universities and relatives.
And whether *I* had a girlfriend and what her breasts
were like—and her mind—and did I like being
subversive, and who would sleep with Nixon? and what was
the name of the motel on route 22 that cost
twenty dollars in 1973, and was it
wrong to prefer the Watergate hearings to making
love, and how the pigs have taken over Doomsday.

Bruce

for Bruce McGrew, 1937–1999

Though if it were a bluebird and not a bunting
I would have been surprised too, nor did he
actually flush the bird out of the pine the way
we did those peacocks in the ditches and fields of
Pennsylvania, but only there were four of us
talking and coming near so *certes* we
disturbed him, maybe brooding, which given
our grand beliefs we would have been a little
ashamed of, *certes* shocked by the sudden burst
of wings and maybe, being humans, surprised
that there were no cries, for we would have cried, and Bruce
did make a little sound, if you knew him you'd know
just what that sound was like and, almost pleading,
he asked us not to tell Fox for she would have missed
her only chance, I almost can hear him, his eyes
did most of the pleading, I know they were gray, we walked
carefully over the stones, there had to be
one or two sticks among us, the bird would have flown
to a safer tree; I kept it from Fox until
we talked on the phone last night, twenty years later.

Grass and Water

The geese have their heaven and I have mine,
though both are made of grass and water and both
have sudden subtle bridges where the carved stone
changes color under the presumptive arches,
and it is microcosmic and symbolic
so I could be there lying under the stars,
if it is one of the hazy afternoons,
and even mistake the birdlime for the Milky Way
or one drop of water in the sunlight
for one of the late afternoons, though nothing I know
will save them even though their eggs are like steel,
even though their guards are wise; whereas I
still am struggling, I with the soft egg, I
with the infantile presidents. You should see me
explaining things to them, below the bridge
this side of the river, not for one good second
ridiculing them. I still am reading and thinking;
I still am comparing; and I am spending my time
like one or two others in *understanding,* that is
a type of heaven too, at least for me it is,
holding on to the stabbed uprooted sycamore.

In Time

As far as clocks—and it is time to think of them—
I have one on my kitchen shelf and it is
flat, with a machine-made flair, a perfect
machine from 1948, at the latest,
and made of shining plastic with the numbers
sharp and clear and slightly magnified in
that heartbreaking postwar style, the cord
too short, though what does it matter, since the mechanism
is broken and it sits unplugged alongside a
cheap ceramic rooster, his head insanely
small and yet his tiny brain alert for
he is the one who will crow and not that broken
buzzing relic, though time is different now
and dawn is different too, you were up all night
and it is dark when he crows and you are waiting
to see what direction you should face and if
you were born in time or was it wasted and what
the day looks like and is the rooster loyal.

Les Neiges d'Antan

Where art thou now, thou Ruth whose husband in the snow
creased thy head with a tire iron, thou who wore
ridiculous hats when they were the rage and loved
exotic cultures and dances such as the *Haitian
Fling* and the *Portuguese Locomotive,* my wife
hated because of her snooty attitude
or that her hair was swept up and her nose was aquiline
and her two boys raised hell with our green apples
the Sunday they came to visit, she in whose Mercury
we parked for over a year, every night
in front of her mother's house in one of the slightly
genteel streets that led into the park
the other side downhill really from the merry-go-round,
or where is Nancy or who is the Nancy Ezra Pound
located in between his racial diatribes
and dry lyrics three times at least in the *Cantos,*
but tell me where that snow is now and tell me—
as in *where is Tangerine* and *where is Flora*—
how old Ruth is and where does she live and does she
still dance the *Locomotive* and does she bundle.

Sink

You can't remember the sink you grew up with
let alone the sink of the year you were born
or the next or the next, and it is always surprising
seeing what an old sink looked like, how shallow
it was, what the spigots were like, how the legs
were merely sticks of sorts, exposed and sodden,
or starting to turn to rust at the broken edges;
and I remember how it was washing my neck
or washing my hair—when I had hair—and how I
had a small sink in one of the rooms I lived in,
though that one hung on the wall and underneath
for I was on the tenth floor or the twentieth,
colored lights went on and off, and there was
a filthy fire escape outside my window on
which I stood by climbing out and I wore
balloon-like shirts for I was completely at home then
wherever I went and I loved day and night
both in and out of my room and it was hopeless
pleasure eating at three or four in the morning and
walking afterwards to one of the bridges
so I could see the still waters before
I went upstairs again to read and sleep.

Mimi

I had to see *La Bohème* again just to
make sure for there was a little part of
me that kept the regret though when I tried
the argument again I used both hands
in order to explain and I was especially
sensitive to the landlord for I lived
both inside and outside and even when I was angry
I paid my debts for I have listened to
and lived with grasshoppers and they bore me, but
Mimi, Mimi, when your hand dropped every
woman in my row was weeping and I
gave in too instead of gripping the armrest
or rubbing the back of my head; I loved it the most that
you lived inside and outside too, the snowdrop
was what you thought of, wasn't it? You were
the one who came back, three times, it was your stubbornness,
your loyalty. One time I stood in the street
and watched a moon so thin the clouds went through it
as if there were no body, as if the cold
was so relentless nothing could live there, you with
the blackened candle, you who stitched the lily.

All I Did for Him

When I fought the dog we almost danced
we loved each other that much and he was strong,
not counting even his teeth and claws, and I had
trouble pushing against him even though his
shoulders were weaker in that position nor was he
intended, as Aristotle might say, for fighting
standing up like that the way maybe a
bear was more intended or certainly an
ape with his gross imitation of a
human, or a human of him, if I can
step into that muck a minute, and he was
taller than me, as I remember, which made him
huge for a dog and made me feel small standing
on two legs with my weak left knee impaired
as it was and smelling his breath and shocked by his giant
head and what had to be a look I never
expected in his eyes, though I had to know
it would be like that for who was I anyhow
to bicker as I did or think that love
as I called it, all I did for him, the food
and water I gave him I could barter, I couldn't
even find my pocket, I couldn't take out a dollar.

Places You Wouldn't Believe

I liked this hotel best because the swimming pool
was on the roof and I was closer by an inch
to the sun that way and there were birds thereby
that fit into the landscape more and flew at
right angles to my elevated body
as I crawled up and down the cement lanes
guided vaguely by the wavering tar; and
I liked the fact that there was a national newspaper
every morning at my door and the rugs were
hideous, and that was that, and they were
poorly laid to boot, I even tripped
and spilled my coffee following the wrong
red arrow once, but I have had an hour
of mercy at the makeshift desk or in the
lobby, such as it was, and I have had mercy
in places you wouldn't believe, so much that I
am ruthless about it; I started with an orange crate
in my living room, and that was that; I know it was
lit up by a brazen dancer with the torches
growing from her belly, my first mercy.

Pag

I didn't know his name yet nor that his eyes
were bulging like that nor that their whites both matched
the white of his handkerchief and the white of his collar,
soft and loose over the double cravat;
nor that there was a purpose to the whites
nor that the knuckles were white as well and that
the strings had popped and he would play on one string
all over Europe and he would be a clown—
at least from time to time—and it was a mas-
querade and it was theatre, he was a type of the
flagrant artist and he would stand for me as
a cipher and the broken violin would
stand as a model for, say, one of my manuscripts
written on shiny butcher paper and I would
do the snapped off strings by telling jokes
and talk in accents—and voices—some kind of stand-up
comedian—I detest the phrase—nobody but
me can say it—for I have a broken string
and I have a handkerchief in my left hand I use to
wipe my neck and pat my cheek and it is
reduced to a wet ball, from pity and anger.

Hydrangea

I was pleased by blue hydrangea because at
last I had a flower from a gorgeous
family I could hate just as when certain
say Jewish poets, whom I'm supposed to revere
because they're Jewish and not to love them would be
an act of betrayal to all eleven prophets;
dozens of kings and clothing manufacturers;
dentists, chess players, swimmers, stockbrokers, English teachers;
psychiatrists, painters, physicists, salesmen, violinists;
social workers, merchants, lawyers, cutters, trimmers;
critics; reveal themselves as snobs and bigots
and analytical and anti-passionate which could be
for all I know another side of Judaism
since Judaism has three sides as in the
Mercy, as in the Exceptions, as in the Melancholies,
which takes me back to the blue hydrangea I see
between an opening in the fence, it looks like
the blue was painted on, I hate it, I also
hate the red carnation, I love the cream
and when it's cone-shaped, I even like the pink,
may God forgive me, Lord of the lost and destitute.

Crosshatching

All this time I was leading another life
and it is clear now which was the shadow and which
was the substance though I particularly hate the word
shadow to describe it since a shadow
itself is a substance and shadows are lovely and stretch
across my lawn at six in the evening and they
take different forms—when it comes to painting—and one
is a mass in the foreground, one is a shade of likeness,
simply defined, a true state of color,
blue or brown, and one is the clear darkness
we screamed about in restaurants but I
preferred above all else the crosshatching
they attached to New York and Chicago buildings,
some of them—in the drawings—two miles high,
rooted in canyons you can't imagine so deep,
and streetcars in the sky and forests above the
clouds and airplanes below the city and rivers
flowing beside the office buildings all with
that one shadow and graveyards where they should be,
close to the sun, the dates in corrupted purple.

Spider

How you like these threads, said white spider
traveling back and forth between two rooms in
Lambertville, New Jersey, his web a work of
art, truly excessive, spit from his soul,
and the first case of any spit, it came from
my own soul since I am a mimic neurotic.
But how you like my steel? You like my window?
You like my big eye waiting? How you like my
chandelier? How you like fate? You like
my silk? Do cover your legs, do tighten
the arms a little, do tighten around the neck.
And how you like my kiss? How about
my rasping bloody tongue? Weren't those herbs
and such like any household, giant unkempt
Russian sage, the better to smell you, my dear,
and spicy rosemary beside the orange and
purple echinacea, all that a little
to placate—though I know you don't believe it,
for nature is nature—your perverted Isaiah
from running around like crazy in the meat markets.

Dandelions

I keep following the dandelion druff and the call of
    the North Tower,
which is what I want to say as one final thing
after the hottest May and the coldest June I can remember,
but what I want to say I can't find words for,
which no one who knows me would ever believe, all
those professors and janitors and salesmen and secretaries—
    not one
could tell me if druff is related to dandruff, though two
out of four said grandfather lion and made the motion of
blowing the white seeds into the air and watched them
float down, and three out of four said Ah, North Tower,
the center of all existence or the last outpost, but what I
meant was rosehips and what I meant to say was
trees in a line and limestone walls or maybe
just thoughtfulness instead or even affection
or maybe sitting on the ground eating a cheese sandwich,
cross-legged in the white and seeded dandelions.

* The first line of this poem is taken from a letter by Alexandra Lynch.

Hats

For the sake of the fleabane growing rose a little
in the white to give it a natural look, almost
a tree with the branches going left and right and
leaves in the lower limbs, the center golden
and fecund there at the side of the yard as if to
apologize, the petals, if those are petals,
thin as threads, I touch my cream-colored hat;
and for the sake of the hat itself, since hats
are holy to any unreformed Jew, I stand
in front of the single rose of Sharon the deer
ignore—as far as eating—and extend
my hand to the blossoms and thank them for their time—
by folding and crushing my hat, my wrists spread out on
my chest, by pushing the brim to the top of my brow
as if I were sweating, by putting the hat on sideways,
then backwards, then with my right hand touching the rear
ribbon and tilting the peak downward, then taking
the crease out—like a derby, then pulling it down
almost to my ears, all this to thank them
for blooming over and over, for not disappearing.

String Bean

A string bean is born every second, *par example,*
and though it doesn't have the brains of a true
sucker, given there is no head nor any
structures of in and out, and except for that
lengthy string no ability to suffer, and
cooked in a trice and hideous in a can
and when one finds its way into a purse
along with tissue, hotel receipts and pieces of
poems we know that sucker is out for blood,
at least a little terror, at least a little
confusion, but I have loved him consistently for his
taste, a string bean has good taste, and you
will love him also once you learn to trust him,
once you learn to eat him a little at a time,
and once you make a decision about the sucker,
and decide to give him an even break since he is
born every minute, in this case every second,
and you have to decide who the sucker is,
tearing apart your wallet, looking for the poem,
looking for the Blue Cross card from Iowa—
you or the bean—and who has the deepest feelings,
and who can sing Beethoven best, and swim underwater.

Large Pots

It's like coming through a chrysanthemum forest
and one of the pots had swollen grapes painted on
and leaves the size of hands, and one had a bird,
and one had a geometric design at first I thought
were Cretan dancers and athletes walking into
a kind of stadium and all together the colors were
reds and golds; specifically they are pink
and perfect rust and perfect orange and they are
starting to turn to straw although it's only
the tenth of October, my former wife's birthday,
one of only five I know including my
own in February. I started to turn to straw
maybe a year ago, maybe less, with humans
it's more complex, it's not a question of dryness
only, but what do I know? I walk from
pot to pot, I walk from straw man to straw man,
I kiss them goodbye, I know I surprise them, *most* people
juke a little when you kiss them, I kiss
mahogany man goodbye, I kiss his wife,
a coral rose, I hold her for nine or ten seconds.

Savel Kliatchko

He is either dead or alive and his father
played cello for the Pittsburgh symphony orchestra
and he introduced me to Kerenski who walked
a little like the czar did, only he kept
his head and lived in New York and spent the evening
hating Trotsky and Lenin, two of the traitors,
two of roomfuls and roomfuls he remembered;
and Savel had first rights to a job I wanted
teaching English to the Minister of Finance
under the crooked prick, Chiang Kai-shek,
his name was Hsu and he detested Marshall,
and lived in Great Neck and kept his daughter hidden.
A year or so later, on Bastille Day,
Savel was escorting a little Canadian
who came to Paris to make her mind up over
a fiancé; I stole her away from sweet Savel
at twelve or one o'clock, give or take,
and loved for one long day on the street of the Butchers,
and returned her, forgive me, to Savel in one whole piece
the year they turned the lights on, two years after
Henry Wallace was defeated and ostracized,
which we have suffered from for fifty years.
Light a candle for him, do one for Savel.

Irishry

Work was the curse of the drinking class, he loved
to say that and, considering the ignorance
of almost everyone about say the last
fifty or hundred years, not to mention just
four, you can't take anything for granted. First,
what was the saying itself and how does my mind
deviate a little or reverse itself,
and would you guess one in twelve knows the original,
and one in forty—or fifty—understands the reversal,
and how many know the songs I sing, is it
one in fifty knows the words, or one in
eighty, even enough to make some sense,
assuming sense was what those songs were about; and
who would know the ladies with the placards, and
who would hear my son and me shouting and
wiping the sweat and tears away in fake
Irishry for only the Irish would say
Drink is the curse of the working class, we never got
tired repeating it, pouring the beer and whiskey.

1940 LaSalle

Did I or didn't I write about Lucky Burkin?
I can't remember; he hired two full sleepers
from the Pennsylvania Railroad—Silver Star,
Silver Torpedo—I'm doing it only by memory—
in '37 or '38, the year the University
of Pittsburgh finally went to the Rose Bowl,
to take his friends—meals, hotels, tickets,
and Pittsburgh won—was it over Washington State?
Lucky was my cousin—I had sixty
on my father's side alone—the two of them sat
in Lucky's 1940 LaSalle coupe, he
called it his office, and talked about business, he wanted
to go legit, no more betting parlors, whore houses,
numbers and loans—he wanted to be my father's
silent partner, money wasn't an issue, but my mother,
who always bet on the wrong horse, didn't want my father
to be connected with a *gonif.* Lucky
went to Florida to lose a hundred pounds
and marry a nice Jewish girl but he
caught pneumonia and died; he had six chins
I think, the money was buried in western Pennsylvania,
Ohio and West Virginia under different names,
his mother was called Gittel, I don't know in English.

Blue Sheets

Look at his moustache now, look at his tragic
face, if he had stayed outside Toulouse
and not come back, if he had stuck with Villon,
his secret holy master, he never should have
been obedient, he would have let the Testaments
keep him alive, and added his own testament
by staying there, he could have rectified his
life through words though he insisted, didn't he,
that life came first; he should have been more stubborn,
he never should have cried, he never should have
written letters onto those thin blue sheets
and licked them shut, nor should he have allowed
his mind to argue with itself that way
nor should he have gone back after only skimming
the surface, as he did, what was he going back to,
a lover he hardly knew? A rigid mother
and father? A school that never missed him? It could have
been Burns, it could have been Hart Crane who had
more than a little of the same obedience,
driven by his lake. I was by rivers.

Iris

The lock was on the right although I had to
open it from the left so I could use
my other hand to turn the knob and there were
four windows facing the street and for a
study I put my feet on the painted board
that covered the radiator and that's where I
slept for an hour since it was too exhausting
to cross the room, and when I got up I walked
downstairs so I could sit in the square on one
of the cold benches behind the limp flags
for it was two in the morning and the prostitutes
were making faces at the slow-moving cop cars
and smoking cigarettes the secondhand smoke of
which I moved two benches away to escape
though I didn't say a word nor did they ask me
for anything more than a cigarette, and one of them
gave me a flower, it was a faded blue iris,
and it was cold that night, I put it inside
my shirt so I could hurry home to adore it.

Grand Hotel

The time I took Anne Marie to what had been
a Nazi brothel in Prague some tourists were standing
under the chandelier and some leftover communist
stood there explaining the thickness of glass and what
the history was of glassmaking in the Czech
Republic, and we walked through them to get
seats so we could suck in the *Art Nouveau*
over our coffee and undercooked pancakes
before we got into the ancient elevator
and went back to our room, *en suite,* as it were,
and dirty, dark, and seedy at that, and looked
in the bottom of the wardrobe, behind the blankets,
to see what they did with love—the pricks—and could
we sleep on that mattress, and how thick was the window glass,
and this time walked down the great marble staircase
holding hands the whole way down, nor did I
bark even once or say *fuck you* to the Germans.

Apocalypse

Of all sixty of us I am the only one who went
to the four corners though I don't say it
out of pride but more like a type of regret,
and I did it because there was no one I truly believed
in though once when I climbed the hill in Skye
and arrived at the rough tables I saw the only other
elder who was a vegetarian—in Scotland—
and visited Orwell and rode a small motorcycle
to get from place to place; and I immediately
stopped eating fish and meat and lived on soups;
and we wrote each other in the middle and late fifties
though one day I got a letter from his daughter
that he had died in an accident; he was
I'm sure of it, an angel who flew in midair
with one eternal gospel to proclaim
to those inhabiting the earth and every nation;
and now that I go through my papers every day
I search and search for his letters but to my shame
I have even forgotten his name, that messenger
who came to me with tablespoons of blue lentils.

Sam and Morris

I had two uncles who were proletarians
and one of them was a house painter and one of them
was a carpenter—they beat their wives
regularly and they had nineteen children
between them. Once a month or so my father
would go to one of their houses to intervene
and once I remember a police car with a dog.
When I was home on a short furlough I went
with my mother and father to a Jewish restaurant
and there, sitting in the back, were my two uncles,
in their seventies by then, and eating together,
chicken, chopped liver, God knows what, but pickles
and cole slaw, there always were pickles and cole slaw
and they were almost conspiring, it seemed to me
then, so young I was, and I was reading my
Ezra Pound already and I was ashamed of
what he said about Jews. Of usury those
two unshaven *yidden,* one of them red-eyed
already from whiskey, they knew nothing, they never
heard of Rothschild. Their hands were huge and stiff,
they hardly could eat their *kreplach,* Pound, you bastard!

Burning

Where is the mind that asked whether the drugstore
that stood at the crest of a hill and had a beacon
as its emblem, and I ate fruit salad sundaes there
and grilled cheese sandwiches, was or wasn't a tower,
in the sense that there were porches, windows and staircases,
in the sense that there were mirrors and shining lamps
and one or two banners, and what was a tower doing there
with me walking to the library and post office,
and only a Chinese restaurant next door;
and where is the mind that abided the large plaza
outside the drugstore and made its own canopies
and beautiful flying objects, and where did the tower
come from and the dream of emptiness
that has abided for more than fifty years,
and the heart which burned, such was burning, and such
was the tower, it also burned, only in that case
it wasn't attached to anything, it burned
of its own volition and mountains in Pennsylvania
still burn, alas, they have an abode, and empty
bottles explode and paper flutes burn and birdsong.

Studebaker

Try a small black radio from any year
and listen to the voices you get, they were
much faster then, they raced ahead of us
and rushed the music; love was in a rocking chair,
the floor was crooked, the moon was already in
the sky, though it was daylight still; or love
was in a Studebaker, we were driving east
and we had no idea how long the corporation
would last, or if there was a corporation, how could we?
And did it have its headquarters in Delaware
for taxes and connections, though the doors
were heavy and solid, what was the year? '55?
The Lark appeared in 1958 or
'59—it was their last attempt,
though I remember the Wagoneer, it was 19-
66 and something called the Cruiser, we had
Nat King Cole on the radio though static
was bad in Pennsylvania, given the mountains,
and there was a lever you pushed to make a bed—
I hope I'm getting it right—the leaves on the windshield
were large and wet, the song was *Unforgettable,*
the tree was either a swamp maple or a sycamore.

Standing Up

This is what happened, and those who want to judge me
can all be damned, my friend Larry was called up
months, years really, before me—1942
I think—and he put me in charge, I don't know
what else to call it, what else to say, of the girl—
I think she was seventeen—he was keeping company with;
she was a K.M., a kitchen mechanic; in the stupid
world we lived in, half the families had maids
from the Slavic world surrounding us; and I was to
be her protector and I was allowed to fuck her
but only standing up, that was the pact the
three of us made, and I was loyal and never
broke the rule, though it was hard on the thighs,
and we grew a little to love each other but I
was always true to Larry. She wore a chenille
robe, a kind of violet, and her breath
always smelled of peanuts; to this day I
smell the peanuts. What should I say? We went
to the movies and took long walks in the woods;
I think they got married after the war and moved
to California. I wish I could say her name.

Cost

From the beginning it was the money, how I
could live on seven dollars a week anywhere
outside the U.S. or go to France
on the G.I. Bill, and learn to love cauliflower.
Although the Caribbean was even cheaper
and Mexico cheaper than that. You wouldn't believe
what life was like after the war, that was
the time, if ever, to live on nothing. I was
enflamed by an article in *Look* magazine,
news went sideways then, but I had already
spent a year in New York City. I was
more or less getting ready, and it was odd
that money would so engross me; I got started
early and it went on for years; I kept
notebooks then as I do now; I love
looking at the stacks of figures, how much
it cost to read Catullus in Latin, what it
cost to understand Villon, including
the price of books and bicycles, not to mention
the price of a lost epic—by week or by month—
and what my ignorance cost and what my stubbornness.

Still Burning

Me trying to understand say whence
say whither, say what, say me with a pencil walking,
say reading the dictionary, say learning medieval
Latin, reading Spengler, reading Whitehead,
William James I loved him, swimming breaststroke
and thinking for an hour, how did I get here?
Or thinking in line, say the 69 streetcar
or 68 or 67 Swissvale,
that would take me elsewhere, me with a textbook
reading the pre-Socratics, so badly written,
whoever the author was, me on the floor of
the lighted stacks and sitting cross-legged,
walking afterwards through the park or sometimes
running across the bridges and up the hills,
sitting down in our tiny diningroom,
burning in a certain way, still burning.

Samaritans

I can't remember what the class trip was —
I think we were going to visit the Samaritans
who lived in round houses at the border of
West Virginia. They believed in a round eye
staring at God, or maybe it was God who had
the eye and stared at them and Moses alone was
the light, as far as they were concerned, and his was
the only law they followed, forget the other
prophets, so-called; and how they got to West Virginia
I forget, though I know our teacher, a specialist
in sociology, was teaching religion
when we went on the trip. I think I got
waylaid a little, the way you did then:
it was spring and warm, the girls had on
light dresses and we had cigarettes, the chimney
holes looked like eyes, but it was God's eye
that I will never forget, it followed the bus
back to Pittsburgh and sometimes it seemed to smile
the way an eye smiles though it was incorporeal
of course and my own eyes were closed—I was sleeping.

Roses

There was a rose called Guy de Maupassant,
a carmine pink that smelled like a Granny Smith
and there was another from the seventeenth century
that wept too much and wilted when you looked;
and one that caused tuberculosis, doctors
dug them up, they wore white masks and posted
warnings in the windows. One wet day
it started to hail and pellets the size of snowballs
fell on the roses. It's hard for me to look at
a Duchess of Windsor, it was worn by Franco
and Mussolini, it stabbed Jews; yesterday I bought
six roses from a Haitian on Lower Broadway;
he wrapped them in blue tissue paper, it was
starting to snow and both of us had on the wrong shoes,
though it was wind, he said, not snow that ruined
roses and all you had to do was hold them
against your chest. He had a ring on his pinky
the size of a grape and half his teeth were gone.
So I loved him and spoke to him in false Creole
for which he hugged me and enveloped me
in his camel hair coat with most of the buttons missing,
and we were brothers for life, we swore it in French.

Letters

These are the letters that go with the picture I have
of Pat and me in Paris in 1955;
I had a turtleneck sweater she knit
with a loose-fitting navy blue or black suit coat
and one of those huge and precious moustaches
that stood for freedom—and arrogance—and there was
a cigarette, in my left hand of course, I held
in perfect knowledge, my wrist was limp, my forehead
was huge and I looked straight ahead at the camera;
Pat had on what looked like a soft wool dress—
I think it was the one with the sleeves cut off
because they itched, or they were too long or bulky,
who knows why? And there was a soft wool collar
to go with the dress, I think it was rust. She looked at me
with adoration—I am ashamed to say—and she was
beautiful. Nor did she have a cigarette,
though *she* was the smoker, Gauloise in France, Woodbines
in Scotland, eventually some black cigars at
home; it was a kind of studio photograph, the
letters are on brown paper tied in a bundle.

The Hammer

What did a foot of snow matter when I
was upstairs with my hammer banging against
the radiators; and what good was my threadbare
camel's hair coat and white silk scarf inside
that freezing office I paid seven dollars a month
for, including heat; and what did it matter that I
grew up on the wrong side of the Alleghenies
and got the news from New York, oh five, ten years
too late, and was the hammer well balanced or not?
And did I wear my coat when I read and did I
wear the scarf like a babushka or wasn't there
a green beret somewhere, and what did my moustache
have to do with it, and wasn't it fine,
that waiting, and wasn't the floor covered with paper
the way a floor should be, a perfect record of
a year or so in that ruined mountain city
where I spoke out on my side of the burned-over slag heap?

Hearts

The larger our hearts were, the more
blurred our love was, the softer
our arrows became, the vaguer
our initials, the deeper
the woods were and more abandoned
the more distant we were and more
absurdly hooked by those arrows
and linked by those bulging valves
whose soft contours were widened
with time and roughened at the edges
whatever you were, whatever
the life was that kept us connected,
buried in a birch too close
for comfort to a black locust
whose one side was destroyed
more than half a century
after we stopped downstream
to look at the stone farmhouse,
a fence holding up a dead
rosebush, another birch
starting to sprout, some clattering
and croaking in both directions.

Ted Rosenberg

And the nineteen poets sitting on their thrones
posed for a picture before the patient photographer
Ted Rosenberg, but the picture would have been
too wide considering there were only two rows
of thrones and the thrones themselves were large, so
he moved us to the wooden steps the left side
of the throne room, and somehow easily
all the poets got into a vertical
position, two or three to a step; on my step
there seemed to be four but when I looked at the feet
there really were two and one of the poets, he standing on
the ground in front and to the side, he had a
cane and there were rows of bicycles to his right
and one of us had a tie, and one of us, me, it
turns out, wore suspenders; and how the others felt
about the picture I don't know but I
felt that we were shadows caught with our mouths
open, staring at nothing. Ted Rosenberg
was himself a shadow, as far as light was concerned,
staring at the others through his Hasselblad.

Slash of Red

It was another one of his petite visions
and he had one every day now—at Optiques,
at Gold and Silver—and he ended up,
for it was hard work, sitting against a wall;
and when he looked at the yard he knew the dimensions
were ancient, *holy* he called them, and made comparisons
to African and Turkish rectangles,
only his yard was bare, there were two trees,
and a brick walk going from the gate to the steps.
He said it was Zen-like, only he meant he resisted
the fountaineers and their computer drawings;
it was a straight line, there wasn't a curve
in the middle, there wasn't a jog at the end,
considering that he never used a string,
and he was proud that he had only a trowel
and a little sand to place the bricks. He counted
320, some broken, some not,
and thought about it as a slash of red
against a background of green. This is how
he entered the twenty-first century. More charitable now.

Salt

I was sitting at a picnic table at
one of the godforsaken places peeling
an egg as if in this act I could recover
what there was of gentleness and I
was alone unless you counted the two forms of life,
one sea and one land, that fought over the eggshells
and stole pieces of bread from each other
with total disregard for the proprieties,
and I abused some rot and pulled out a screw
that hardly held itself in place; I could have
rocked the table with my hands, such was
the purchase; and the woods were birch, cattails
down below, a train sliding slowly
past the stone station, up above me;
and what I missed was salt, for I had wine
and even a tomato, I should have taken
one of the beautiful cellars from my shelf
and put it in my pocket or wrapped it in foil
and packed it in the bag, it would have made
the animals happier, it would have blessed our supper.

Egg

And I have been a mother to geese and what not,
I hired forty-five poets in Pennsylvania
and sent them to the northern and western reaches
after I trained them at Lewisburg during the summer
institute and visited the schools and
traveled in an old Toyota in all the
sixty-seven counties and lived in a hotel in
Harrisburg three days a week and talked to them
about love and money and teaching and poetry;
and I was the head of a teachers' union and I was
a chair, as we say, and I bought the food for my own
family and I did the Band-Aids, and I gave
advice in three or four cities, and there was a small
goose who followed me everywhere, honking with love,
and I was exhausted; I hated him, always on top
of me—I wanted to kick him—my third child!—
He was a machine, food on one end, shit on the
other—and there was an egg I had to break with a
hammer, I paid a quarter for it, the omelette was
orange, and huge, I was so hungry then.

Box of Cigars

I tried either one or two but they were stale
and broke like sticks or crumbled when I rolled them
and lighting a match was useless nor could I
put them back in the refrigerator—
it was too late for that—even licking them
filled my mouth with ground-up outer leaf,
product of Lancaster or eastern Virginia,
so schooled I am with cigars, it comes in the blood,
and I threw handfuls of them into the street
from three floors up and, to my horror, sitting
on my stoop were four or five street people
who ran to catch them as if they were suddenly rich,
and I apologize for that, no one should
be degraded that way, my hands were crazy,
and I ran down to explain but they were smoking
already nor did I have anything to give them
since we were living on beans ourselves, I sat
and smoked too, and once in a while we looked
up at the open window, and one of us spit
into his empty can. We were visionaries.

Justice

Only, to hear him scream, you had to know
that he was in the body of the worm
and even the robin could hear the scream, so close
she was to the shaking ground, and though the struggle
was over in less than a minute, the sun turned red,
as you could see between the birches, but that
was just a decoration, a brief statement
as on a gravestone, *Here lies such and such,*
and at the bottom, below a lily, *the worm*
will lie down with the robin, or it was
two carved roses intertwined, or maybe
the sun was more pink, more from shame, it only
lasted a few seconds considering the
size of things, and more and more the hopping
and screaming, whatever he was, however he was
dismembered, and as for justice, it was redder
still, you would say carmine, you would say ruby,
my clothes were red, my neck and face were scarlet.

American Heaven

A salt water pond in the Hamptons near David
Ignatow's house, the water up to my chest,
an American Heaven, a dog on the shore, this time
his mouth closed, his body alert, his ears
up, a dog *belongs* in heaven, at least our
kind. An egret skidding to a stop, I'm sure
water snakes and turtles, grasses and weeds,
and close to the water sycamores and locusts,
and pitch pine on the hill and sand in the distance,
and girls could suckle their babies standing in water,
so that was our place of origin, that was
the theory in 1982—David
had his own larder, Rose had hers, he brought
tuna fish into her kitchen, it was a triptych,
the centerpiece was the pond, the left panel
was his, his study, and he was stepping naked
across the frame into the pond holding an
open can and hers was the right, her arms had
entered the pond, holding a bowl, it was her
studio, we ate on a dry stone
and talked about James Wright and Stanley Kunitz,
and there was a star of the fourth magnitude
surrounded by planets, shining on all of us.